90 DAYS PAYS

By a Grateful Recovering Alcoholic

QUOTIDIAN PUBLISHERS
CUSHING, MAINE
2012

90 Days Pays
Copyright © 2012
By the Anonymous Author
(Formerly "My First Ninety Days")

Available through

www.createspace.com/3938271

www.amazon.com

and

QUOTIDIAN PUBLISHERS
(One-day-at-a-time in Latin)
377 River Road
Cushing, ME 04563
Phone 207-809-1167

COVER TITLE:
STEPPING STONES

Symbolic of the Twelve Steps of
Alcoholics Anonymous,
recognizing that Bill Wilson,
co-founder of AA, and his wife Lois,
named their home in Bedford Hills, NY
"Stepping Stones."

TRY NINETY IN NINETY

Dear Friend:

This little diary can help you through the first 90 days free of alcohol and other mood-altering substances. "The Program" is any Anonymous Twelve Step program.

This booklet is NOT a substitute for meetings or talking every day with your sponsor and friends in your Fellowship, but reading just one page each morning may help to set your thinking in a positive direction.

Are you too bored or complaisant with the Program or just coming back? Did you build an immunity to its simple truths by talking the talk instead of walking the walk? Welcome back! Ninety days pays in so many ways! You can make it! Millions of us are making it along with you, one day at a time. It's a serene and beautiful life.

A Recovering Alcoholic

This book not formally approved by any Program.

The 1st DAY

People are saying to me, "Welcome to the Fellowship." It's begun to dawn on me that my addiction rules *me,* not the other way around. I can't predict how I'll behave once I take something. My life's messed up. They tell me I'm taking the FIRST STEP toward recovery. All I know is that I feel better admitting out loud to someone that I have a problem!

STEP ONE:

"We admitted we were powerless over alcohol (our addiction); that our lives had become unmanageable."

The 2nd DAY

Program People (I'm going to call them People in Recovery or PIRs for short) are understanding. They're telling me I can make it just the way they're making it. It's *simple,* they say. Just don't take the *first* one.

Yes, that's simple, all right...

Doesn't sound easy, though!

DON'T TAKE THE FIRST SIP, GULP, BITE, DROP, POP, SHOT, SNORT OR PUFF.

The 3rd DAY

I'm not sure I know what I'm getting into. They're suggesting that I go to

NINETY MEETINGS IN

NINETY DAYS.

Whew!

That's a lot, don't you think? I wonder what all that sitting around and talking is going to do for me.

But if I used every day, PIRs tell me I can *use the Program every day* instead.

There's a lot of meetings around. Maybe I can do it.

The 4th DAY

Am I anxious and jittery! My head's foggy! PIRs are telling me I'm *going through withdrawal*, and I'm sure to feel lousy until my body adjusts to being clean, sober and abstinent. They've all been through it, and they say it's natural.

I've tried to quit by myself before and it didn't work, so this time I'm going to listen.

And if they think I should go to a detox, I'll go.

Right now, feeling rotten's bearable because they're telling me

IT GETS BETTER!

The 5th DAY

I keep hearing "Do it one hour – or even one *minute* – at a time if necessary. The craving will pass." I thought they were nuts, but it's beginning to make sense. The way I see it, I don't have to give in to my addiction today.

Forget about tomorrow. This day is all that counts.

What a relief! I never thought of it that way before.

**TAKE IT
ONE DAY AT A TIME.**

The 6th DAY

I can't sleep! I've been tossing and turning until all hours. I think I should take "just a little something" to help me, but PIRs can be awfully blunt. They just say "NO!" and tell me I'll be okay.

They just keep smiling and remind me:

NOBODY EVER DIED FROM LACK OF SLEEP!

I got some other advice about sleeping too. Get up a*t the very same time every morning – even if I've only slept a couple of hours*. This will help me set a *normal* sleep pattern.

When was the last time I felt normal?

The 7th Day

Hey! It's been a whole week! Amazing! I mentioned at my meeting that I'd been clean and sober now for seven days. They all applauded. Really! That gives me hope.

Now they're reminding me to

GET PHONE NUMBERS AND USE THEM.

I don't like to bother people with my problems, but they're saying they really *want* to hear from me *before* I take something. What can they do over the phone to help me?

But if this is what it's going to take, I'll do it. One phone call, at least one, every single day!

The 8th DAY

I've been thinking about the Second Step: "Came to believe that a Power *greater than ourselves* could restore us to sanity." I know I've been crazy, but I'm not sure about this power-greater-than-myself.

PIRs suggest that I lean on my Group for now. You know, it IS powerful! I always feel better at a meeting – and afterwards, too. I feel stronger about staying away from that first one. When I tried doing it alone I failed over and over.

Yes, they're more powerful than I am. It makes sense to do it together.

USE THE POWER OF THE GROUP.

The 9th DAY

I've been doing a lot of thinking about the Program. Who am I doing this for? Who cares if I get clean and sober?

I joined the Program to get people and troubles off my back. It's different now. When I'm at a meeting I see smiling faces. They're not faking; they *like* what's happening to them. Me too. I'm the only one I have to satisfy.

I'M MAKING A COMMITMENT TO <u>MYSELF</u>.

The 10th DAY

IT'S TIME TO GET A SPONSOR

I've been thinking about the kind of person I want—the relationship has to be gut-level honest, but I think I'm a little afraid of that. And I've been listening when PIRs speak. My sponsor has to be *living* the Program—walking the walk, not just talking the talk.

I'm scared to ask, but I already know who I want. All I have to do is get over this fear of rejection! I'll do it. I'm going to ask this person tonight!

The 11th DAY

I can't help thinking the slogans are kind of silly. Too simple to help with *my* complicated life! But in the last few days I've been saying them to myself when problems come up, and it's working.

EASY DOES IT!

This slows me down a little and gives me time to make a good decision. I'm not spinning my wheels quite so much.

The 12th DAY

I just learned there's another part to that slogan, "Easy Does it."

BUT DO IT!

Oops! Why is it I know exactly what I need to do, but I keep stalling anyway?

I'm going to a meeting tonight and get a sponsor!

The 13th DAY

Even when nothing much happens, I usually feel better after I've been to a meeting. Then I get home and sometimes I can't sleep. My sponsor says go light on the coffee and don't worry.

MEETINGS ARE A "NATURAL HIGH!"

I can just sit back, relax and listen -- and enjoy the good feelings.

A natural high—it's something to think about, isn't it?

The 14th DAY

My sponsor seems to have an answer for everything! I said "I don't have a favorite meeting. They're all okay."

Right away I was told to

GET A HOME GROUP

and attend its meetings every week without fail – not to mention learn every-one's name, set up chairs, pick up cups and attend the business meetings.

I finally got it. I'm supposed to make it *my* group!

The 15th DAY

I've been thinking about taking just a little something. The craving's getting stronger, and a voice in my head's been whispering, "Just one won't hurt you." I'm getting upset, so I made it the topic of my meeting. You know what they came up with?

THINK IT THROUGH!

I've been trying so hard NOT to think about it, but they're saying just the opposite. I'm supposed to look my addiction straight in the eye – from the first good feeling through all the changes right to the misery at the end.

Hey, it *does* make a difference in my attitude. I don't ever want to go back there!

The 16th DAY

Today the Program gave me a new tool for staying clean and sober, The word is HALT. It stands for 4 things I ought to avoid:

DON'T GET TOO <u>H</u>UNGRY, <u>A</u>NGRY, <u>L</u>ONELY OR <u>T</u>IRED.

Any one of these can lead me back to drinking or drugging. So how do I avoid these troublemakers? Simple, they say: Eat regularly, talk to my sponsor honestly, go to meetings and get to bed on time. They're treating me like a kid!

Or maybe it's about growing up and taking responsibility for myself. It's hard work.

The 17th DAY

The things I'm learning in the Program are so new! I don't know if I believe everything I'm hearing.

But I notice that everyone who follows the Program and attends meetings regularly is doing okay. They're telling me to try it wholeheartedly for 3 months.

IF I DON'T LIKE THE PROGRAM AFTER 90 DAYS, THEY'LL GLADLY REFUND MY MISERY!

The 18th DAY

I'm supposed to go to a family affair in a couple of weeks. I feel anxious every time I think of it. There'll be a lot of drinking and drugging. With my family there always is! And they all like to tell me what I'm doing wrong.

My sponsor says I don't have to go. I never would've thought of that. Choose not to attend!

My sponsor says:

**I MUST
PROTECT MY SOBRIETY
ABOVE EVERYTHING ELSE.**

The 19th DAY

Now that I'm feeling surer of myself, I've decided to visit some old "buddies." (Planning to refuse everything they offer me!) When I mentioned my decision at a meeting, they all reminded me that my old "friends" only get together for one purpose – to get high. I don't belong any place where that's the main focus – like a Bar. They said:

IF YOU DON'T WANT TO GET HIT BY A TRAIN, DON'T SIT ON THE TRACKS!

I had to admit it made sense, so I'm going for coffee with some PIRs instead.

The 20th DAY

Today I was beginning to believe that my drinking and drugging were really okay. After all, I've heard much worse stories than mine at speaker meetings. I wasn't *that* bad, I was telling myself.

But then I remembered that the leader usually says, "Sit back, relax and listen:

IDENTIFY, DON'T COMPARE!"

I certainly identify with the feelings like fear, anger, resentment, self-pity and remorse. I think I'd better do what I'm told. Instead of telling myself "I didn't do *that*," *I'm getting to the truth: I felt the same way everyone else did!*

The 21st DAY

Three whole weeks today! Clean and sober! I don't know how it happened, but it feels so good. I was beginning to tell myself, "See, I can handle it; maybe I don't really have a problem." But my sponsor says

WATCH OUT FOR STINKIN' THINKIN'!

My sponsor says that's just my addiction whispering lies in my ear.

I'd better get to a meeting.

The 22nd DAY

I've been wondering why I must go to so many meetings. What do they do for me? I'm feeling better, but they're interrupting my life.

Uh oh! I can hear my new friends reminding me that meetings are vital—the medicine for my disease. At the same time they say, *"The number of meetings you attend is strictly up to you!"*

Then they suggest that I

<u>CHOOSE</u> TO GO TO A MEETING, JUST FOR TODAY

That means I can stop thinking crazy thoughts like "Do I have to go to meetings for the rest of my life?" All I do is choose what's good for me t*oday*. Tomorrow isn't here yet!

The 23rd DAY

Some of my old "using" friends are telling me all I have to do is forget the past and just limit myself to "social" drinking or drugging.

I'm beginning to realize I honestly can't do that. With me, it's all or nothing! My sponsor says I need to remember that truth, and

KEEP MY MEMORY GREEN

by remembering what I was really like. It's too easy to forget, because I don't like to think about the misery and pain I brought on myself and other people.

The 24ᵗʰ DAY

What kind of meetings shall I go to? Sometimes I like speakers' meetings, because I can sit back, relax and listen. But I'm getting good ideas from my discussion meetings too. And right now my favorite is a meeting for just my own sex – the talk's more open than in a mixed group, and I get the support I need.

My sponsor says it's never too soon to start Step meetings.

I guess I need a little bit of everything.

CHOOSE A MIX OF MEETINGS FOR EVERY WEEK.

The 25th DAY

Program people are forever talking about "working the steps," so I asked my sponsor about it. I was told I'm too new in the Program; the rest of the Steps can wait until I've celebrated 90 days at least. I just have to stick with the first three Steps. This is the simple form:

STEP ONE: I CAN'T;
STEP TWO: HE CAN;
STEP THREE: I'LL LET HIM.

Some people have trouble with the idea of a Higher Power. My sponsor said that's okay. Make it the <u>G</u>uidance <u>O</u>f <u>D</u>runks instead.

I can't, <u>they</u> can; so I'll let <u>them</u> guide me. I get it!

The 26ᵀᴴ DAY

PIRs—People in Recovery, that is—keep asking me what *I* want. I'm supposed to consider what's right for <u>me</u>.

I wasn't brought up to think of myself first. Isn't that being selfish?

But I'm being told that I <u>must</u> be self-caring (not self-centered) if I want to be clean, serene, abstinent, sober and healthy.

They're pretty clear about it:

IT'S A SELFISH PROGRAM!

The 27th DAY

Family and old friends aren't necessarily supporting my sobriety. They don't really understand addiction, so I'm getting all kinds of advice that may not be good for me right now.

The Program has a slogan to remind me where I belong:

**STICK
WITH THE WINNERS!**

That means people who are staying clean, sober and abstinent one day at a time, going to meetings and working on themselves.

Sounds like good advice to me!

The 28th DAY

Holidays and family ceremonies always seem to be coming up. They're not happy times for me—I usually feel anxious, depressed and pressured. But I've discovered that meetings *never* take a holiday, and some groups have twenty-four hour meetings then, just in case I'm alone and need sober companionship.

That's reassuring.

My sponsor says I can leave a holiday party if I feel uncomfortable—or not go at all. I <u>do</u> have choices.

STICK CLOSE TO PROGRAM PEOPLE ON HOLIDAYS.

The 29th DAY

I'm beginning to understand I truly have a disease and not a moral problem—even though the behavior brought on by my addiction was certainly unacceptable.

My disease has many symptoms that can be predicted and described. One is "Denial." I'm still experiencing it. My mind forgets the reality of my addiction.

**I HAVE A DISEASE
THAT TELLS ME
I DON'T HAVE A DISEASE!**

The 30th DAY

A whole month clean and sober! Some days, staying straight is a snap; other times I'm barely hanging on by my fingernails. So every morning, just after waking up, I repeat a promise to myself. It helps me keep a positive attitude. It's a form of the First Step:

I'M POWERLESS OVER DRUGS AND ALCOHOL. TODAY I WILL STAY CLOSE TO THE PROGRAM.

Then I find time to read some Program literature or phone my sponsor. We may only talk a couple of minutes, but that daily contact sets my mind in a sober direction.

The 31st DAY

Once an addict, always an addict. It's been hard for me to accept that fact. When I give my name at meetings, I want so much to say "I *was*, but not anymore!"

Program people know the truth and they say it with a tangy bit of humor:

ONCE YOU'VE BEEN A PICKLE, YOU CAN NEVER BE CUCUMBER AGAIN!

The 32nd DAY

At the beginning of each meeting, the leader reads the Preamble. It points out that

I'VE JOINED A FELLOWSHIP OF MEN AND WOMEN WHO SHARE THEIR EXPERIENCE, STRENGTH AND HOPE WITH EACH OTHER.

That means I have to take part in the discussions as honestly as I can, even if I don't have much to say. I can't just sit back and be an observer, no matter how much I hate speaking up in a group.

The 33rd DAY

IT TAKES TIME.

I don't want to hear that phrase again. They say it over and over, and I'm getting impatient. I want my life to get better *right now*, and it's not working out.

In fact, some parts of my life are getting worse. But I can see a difference. People who've been clean and sober for a while are much more relaxed than the newcomers.

I have to believe them; they've been right about everything so far.

T.I.M.E. Things I Must Earn.

The 34th DAY

The farther away I get from my last drink or drug, the more things I remember that I want to forget. I've been doing my best to put them out of my mind, but at meetings I've been told just the opposite:

HE WHO FORGETS IS DOOMED TO REPEAT.

They want me to remember what it was like so I can learn from my past. It's not fun to recall all that trouble and pain. But I don't ever want to go back. At least I know that much!

The 35th DAY

Whenever a drink or a drug flashed through my mind, I'd push it away fast by thinking of something pleasant. But my sponsor says that's a dangerous practice. It's really training my mind to think "Drug = good."

Instead, right away I ought to bring to mind *the most distasteful experience I can remember during my active addiction,* so my mind will learn to link the negative.

DRINK/DRUG = gross, bad, repulsive, disgusting, or shameful, embarrassing, sickening...

I can add my own negative words right here too!

My mind is naturally selective. I'd rather remember the good times. Now I'm learning to remember an awful experience, and it's working. Already those "good times" are less appealing.

TIME

This Is Me Evolving!

The 36th DAY

I didn't realize how much time I spent surrounding myself with drinking or drugging activities. Now I'm talking to Program people to find out what they do to fill up their lives.

I'm discovering my own interests at last. It takes work and creativity to build a new life.

I'M FILLING MY LIFE WITH SOBER ACTIVITIES.

The 37th DAY

I feel so guilty remembering the rotten things I did when I was drunk or drugged.

People in the Fellowship tell me not to beat myself up over it; later I can follow the suggestions of the Twelve Steps and make amends. In the meantime, I need to pat myself on the back for taking positive steps in my life *today*.

THE WORST DAY SOBER IS BETTER THAN THE BEST DAY DRUNK OR DRUGGED.

The 38th DAY

I get so angry whenever I remember all the lousy and unfair things other people have done to me.

The Program deals a lot with these resentments, and I've brought them up as a discussion topic. That's been good for me. I've gotten lots of ideas on how to get rid of them. They only hurt *me*, after all, and in time might push me to pick up.

I CAN'T AFFORD RESENTMENTS!

The 39th DAY

I can get to feeling so bad about my life—like nothing's going right and nobody understands me.

I'm learning self-pity is the other side of resentment, and when I feel really sorry for myself, I'm just getting stuck.

My sponsor says, get moving and get to a meeting.

DON'T WALLOW IN SELF-PITY; IT'S AN EXCUSE FOR INACTION.

The 40th DAY

I can't help puzzling about the Program. I've started asking a lot of questions like "What if..." and "How come..." and "Why can't I...?" and Program people just chuckle.

They say there's a simple answer for me: "KISS." They even say it with a smile. Sometimes it makes me mad, but I have to trust them. They haven't led me wrong yet.

Keep It Simple, Stupid!

The 41st DAY

Such a huge weight has been lifted from my shoulders! I feel like I can't do anything wrong. The Program's perfect; the Fellowship's perfect. I'm high on life and getting higher every day!

But PIRs are warning me there's such a thing as TOO high. Riding on a pink cloud isn't reality, and some day I'll have to come down. To avoid crashing, they're telling me to double up on the number of meetings I'm going to right now and get more phone numbers and talk to more people.

WHEN I COME OFF MY PINK CLOUD, I WANT to LAND WITH BOTH FEET in the PROGRAM!

The 42nd DAY

We say the Serenity Prayer together at every meeting. I wasn't paying much attention at first, and didn't know the words. But now I repeat it to myself whenever my life starts to unravel. It reminds me I can only change *myself,* not other people, places or things.

**GOD, GRANT ME
THE SERENITY
TO ACCEPT THE THINGS
I CANNOT CHANGE,
COURAGE TO CHANGE
THE THINGS I CAN
AND WISDOM TO KNOW
THE DIFFERENCE.**

The 43rd DAY

I've been getting flak from family and old friends about being around the Program too much. They're telling me other obligations come first. But do they?

I'm beginning to realize my sobriety has to come before everything else. If I'm not clean and sober, I can't cope.

At my meeting, that message came through loud and clear. Sobriety comes <u>before</u> family, friends, money, kids, hobbies – it comes before everyday living. No, that's not right. For me, it IS everyday living!

SOBRIETY IS THE FIRST PRIORITY.

The 44th DAY

I keep hearing the same things over and over. Sometimes I think I'm in kindergarten. Certainly I'm starting at the beginning—and I keep forgetting the simplest principles.

The principles of the Program DO work when I pay attention.

I've been told it's time for me to become open-minded and teachable. I must admit that *my* way wasn't working!

IT'S A SIMPLE PROGRAM FOR COMPLICATED PEOPLE!

The 45th DAY

I'm learning there's a big difference between *compulsion* and *obsession*. *Compulsion* is the gnawing physical craving I get for a drink or drug—that shakiness, anxiety and confusion I feel when I don't get it right away—when every cell in my body is crying out. It can last minutes or even hours.

I'm told that if I don't give in to the compulsion, it will eventually go away and stay away. It's a relief to know the feeling won't last forever.

They've promised me:

THE COMPULSION WILL BE TAKEN FROM ME.

The 46th DAY

Obsession is different, because it lasts much longer and it's "all in my head," But that doesn't make it any less miserable!

Obsession is all those whirling, crazy thoughts of getting high—dreaming about it, planning for it and imagining the release of it. Obsession crowds out every other thought. Nothing else is important. In some ways it's more dangerous than a physical compulsion, but they promise that it too will fade away.

PIRs tell me to talk about it, go to plenty of meetings, listen to my sponsor and *do what the Program tells me to do.*

THE OBSESSION WILL BE LIFTED FROM ME.

THE 47th DAY

The obsession to drink or drug will leave me all the faster if I'm paying attention to the Third Step:

"Made a decision to turn our will and our lives over to the care of God as we understand Him."

I can say to my Higher Power, "Here—You take this obsession; I can't handle it anymore." My sponsor says it has everything to do with willingness.

LET GO AND LET GOD.

The 48th DAY

I've been feeling down lately. The early excitement about sobriety has worn off. Nothing looks good. I don't care what's going on. Nothing's important. I'd just as soon sit home and watch TV.

But my sponsor says, "Lets nip that depression in the bud," and insists on picking me up for a meeting, saying, "You need to get moving *now,* because feeling down could lead you back to your DOC. (That's rehab talk for Drug of Choice.)

TO AVOID DEPRESSION, MOVE OFF THE SPOT!

The 49ᵗʰ DAY

My sponsor says that most newcomers are typical examples of "Self-will run riot" – always wanting our way right away.

I think that's true. How do I get out of that spontaneous trouble? By using another simple, mind-stopping slogan:

THINK!

It's already gotten my mind to slow down just a little.

The 50th DAY

IT'S A PROGRESSIVE DISEASE

I didn't know what that meant the first time I heard it. My sponsor says an addictive disease *continues to progress even if I'm clean and sober*.

Suppose I stop using now, and stay abstinent for years. It's like taking a train from San Francisco to New York and getting off at Salt Lake City. When I pick up again years later, the train of progression has kept on moving without me, so I get on again in Chicago. All the physical, mental and spiritual troubles will catch up with me very fast, and I'll be as sick as if I never stopped at all!

Program people confirm this from their own miserable experiences.

That's really frightening!

There's a lot more to this disease than I ever realized.

The 51st DAY

I've been hearing about people trying "the great experiment" or having a "slip" and finding it hard to come back. I was beginning to think I had to go out and try it again, too. It sounded like *everyone* was doing it.

Then I learned it was just my stinkin' thinkin' again.

Some people never make it back to the Program. They may end up in jail, institutionalized or dead instead.

My sponsor says it this way: *"Don't let the coats get you – the blue, the white or the black."*

They say that if I'm willing to work the Program and listen, I'll stay clean and sober. "Rarely have we seen a person fail who has thoroughly followed our path."

RELAPSE IS <u>NOT</u> A REQUIREMENT!

The 52nd DAY

When I'm getting upset about some serious crisis in my life, and I take the problem to my sponsor or a meeting for some help, they listen and they seem to understand, but I don't get sympathy.

I probably don't need much sympathy anyhow because I've got enough self-pity for two, but why do I get the same simple-minded answer?

Do I *need* to be reminded that picking up will only make it worse?

Probably I do.

"DON'T DRINK OR DRUG..."

The 53rd DAY

". . . AND GO TO MEETINGS."

I'm beginning to understand. If I stay clean and sober and listen to the good, clear, calm thinking of other sober people, I'm eventually going to learn more mature ways of doing things. Why don't they say so?

A couple of days ago I was talking to a real newcomer, and I found myself confidently reassuring him with that same simple answer to all his problems: "Don't drink and go to meetings."

I said it because it works.

The 54th DAY

IT'S A THREEFOLD DISEASE: PHYSICAL, MENTAL AND SPIRITUAL.

Physically, my disease can lead to increased tolerance, acute withdrawal, chronic illness and even brain damage.

Mentally, it can result in memory loss, depression, paranoia or extreme rage, to mention just a few.

Spiritually, I may decide I'm worthless, my life is pointless, my Higher Power has vanished and all sense of right and wrong have been erased.

I won't care for people I once loved and who still love me.

Yes, it's a devastating disease, but with the help of my Higher Power and the Program it *can be arrested*.

The 55th DAY

I've been complaining to everyone in the Program about all the unjust and unfair things other people did to me, especially when I was in my active addiction. As usual, I got no sympathy from any of them. Instead, I got a new way of looking at life:

WHENEVER I POINT A FINGER AT SOMEONE ELSE, THREE FINGERS ARE POINTING BACK AT ME!

The 56TH DAY

I've been wondering just how the Program works.

People who have never been able to stay clean and sober before, no matter how hard they tried, are doing just fine! It's like a miracle! All we do is get together and talk and things get better.

I made the mistake of asking my sponsor how it works.

I had to laugh. My sponsor looked me in the eye and answered seriously:

"IT WORKS VERY WELL."

The 57th DAY

I'm not sure I belong in this Program. I'm not sure I'm an alcoholic and addict; the answers come too slowly and I have a lot of unanswered questions. Besides, I'm expected to be responsible for my Program, my beliefs, my recovery, the number of meetings I attend—*everything!*

No one pushes me to believe or do anything because, they say, "It's a Program of attraction, not promotion." I keep hearing:

BRING THE BODY AND THE MIND WILL FOLLOW!

The 58th DAY

Before I go anywhere, I should know exactly how I'm going to refuse a drink of alcohol. (Yes, I've been reminded that alcohol is a legal drug.) I've been told to come up with an answer that's comfortable for me, and even practice it ahead of time. I would never have thought of doing that!

My group says I'm a sitting duck for trouble if I haven't planned what to say. That makes sense to me. First I came up with all kinds of little white lies, but they didn't sound convincing, even to me. Now I've got a simple, solid, workable answer:

**THANK YOU, NO! OR...
YES! COFFEE NOW, PLEASE.**

The 59th DAY

I've heard the word "surrender" quite a bit. At first I couldn't understand

SURRENDER TO WIN

But finally it was explained to me this way: as long as I'm doing battle with my addiction, I can't get on with the other aspects of my life. If I quit fighting, accept defeat and lay down my weapons of denial and stubbornness and pride—if I stop trying to prove I have control when I don't—then, paradoxically, I WIN!

The 60th DAY

I've been clean and sober for two months! Time is going by so fast! I still remind myself every single morning that I'm powerless over alcohol and drugs. Some days it's very easy to stay away; some days it's so hard I want to give up the Program. My sponsor says I'm exactly where I'm supposed to be in my recovery right now and I'll be more comfortable if I do the program one day at a time.

The progression of healthy acceptance goes like this:

**I *CAN'T DRINK OR DRUG.*
I *WON'T* DRINK OR DRUG.
I DON'T DRINK OR DRUG.**

The 61st DAY

I will always have a threefold disease: physical, mental and spiritual.

First my spirituality was damaged, then my mind, and last my body. As I recover, I regain these aspects of my life in reverse order—first my body, then my mind, and finally my spiritual self.

They tell me

**FIRST I CAME,
THEN I CAME TO.
AT LAST I CAME TO BELIEVE.**

The 62nd DAY

I used to think there were all kinds of good reasons for my drinking and drugging—to celebrate an occasion, to overcome stress or depression, to reward myself, to relax or party—or because it rained, my car broke down, my team won or lost, because of my terrible childhood, my promotion, my divorce.

Now, finally, I understand what my PIRs are telling me:

THERE ARE <u>NO</u> REASONS FOR DRINKING OR DRUGGING, ONLY <u>EXCUSES!</u>

The 63rd DAY

I'm learning so many new things in this wonderful Program!

One is that I must stay free of *all* mood-altering chemicals, whether or not I ever took them before, or thought I was hooked on them—even the sneaky ones like mouthwash and cough medicine with alcohol, or over-the-counter meds and sleeping pills.

The truth is that most anything might trigger my addiction, so they're telling me to

LIVE <u>TOTALLY</u> CLEAN AND SOBER!

The 64th DAY

I'm back to wondering just how this Program works. What makes it tick? How come so many of us are staying clean and sober and putting our lives back together?

As always, my sponsor has an answer for me, reminding me of all the effort we put into changing ourselves.

THE PROGRAM DOESN'T WORK;

I DO!

The 65TH DAY

I know so many people who need this Program! I asked some PIRs how to go about getting <u>them</u> clean and sober. All I wanted was the right words to say!

They finally talked some sense into me, letting me know that my own clean and sober behavior is the best adver-tisement. Each of us has to decide for ourselves whether or not to take that big step.

IT'S A PROGRAM OF ATTRACTION, NOT PROMOTION.

The 66th DAY

I always thought of myself as an honest person, until I started listening to PIRs on the topic. Of course I couldn't help identifying!

Now I realize that I cheated, lied, stole, made believe, denied, minimized, avoided ... and on and on.

My sponsor says it's okay. I only have to recover in the present, and being honest begins *right now*.

IT'S AN HONEST PROGRAM.

The 67th DAY

I'm really feeling good! My life's going better, I'm getting along with people, my head is clearer and I'm making better decisions. I think it's time for me to grab hold of my life and do the things my addiction kept me from doing.

But my sponsor says, "Whoa!" Early sobriety's more fragile than I realize. The Program hasgood advice:

DON'T MAKE ANY MAJOR CHANGES FOR THE FIRST YEAR.

They haven't steered me wrong yet, so I'm going to listen, though I'm not quite sure I believe it—in my special case!

The 68th DAY

I told my sponsor I can begin to cut back on meetings now, because I really understand the Program. My life is going great and my compulsion is gone. I believe I can relax a little now.

My sponsor told me in no uncertain terms to get to a meeting. *Complacency* and *arrogance* are two of the most dangerous symptoms on the smooth road toward a slip. I seem to have forgotten already that

ALCOHOL AND DRUGS ARE CUNNING, BAFFLING, POWERFUL...AND PATIENT!

The 69th DAY

This is a very mysterious and marvelous program. I don't have to sign up for membership or even take a pledge. *I'm a member whenever I say I am!* There's not another organization anywhere that runs like this—a miraculous, worldwide Fellowship!

THE ONLY REQUIREMENT FOR MEMBERSHIP IS A DESIRE TO STOP DRINKING AND DRUGGING.

That means I'm welcome even *before* I get clean and sober–and even when I'm not welcome anywhere else! It feels like I'm coming home.

The 70th DAY

This Program is built on *trust*. It's my job to maintain everyone else's anonymity. I can tell anyone that I'm a member, but it's my responsibility not to mention to outsiders who I've seen here: no names, no histories. That makes everyone feel safe and comfortable. And I don't have to tell anyone about my membership in the Program unless I believe they have a real need to know.

WE PROTECT EACH OTHER'S ANONYMITY.

THE 71st DAY

I've discovered that I can go almost anywhere in the world and find a meeting. And I've begun to realize I must not only care for myself, I must also care for my fellow addicts. That's how it works.

WHENEVER ANYONE, ANYWHERE, REACHES OUT FOR HELP, I WANT THE HAND OF THE PROGRAM ALWAYS TO BE THERE. AND FOR THAT

I AM RESPONSIBLE!

The 72nd DAY

**I MUST LEARN
TO LOVE MYSELF.**

To tell the truth, I haven't been very lovable for the past few years.

My sponsor says not to worry; they'll love me until I can love myself. Just staying clean and sober is a lovable act. Besides, I can make changes in myself that make me more loving and lovable.

The topics at meetings are helping me to see myself honestly, and I know *change is possible*.

The 73rd DAY

There are lots of single people in the Program. As I get healthier, I need to be paid attention to, that's all there is to it! I thought my sponsor was just an old prude, telling me to

AVOID EMOTIONAL INVOLVEMENTS FOR THE FIRST YEAR!

I was furious! I brought it up at a meeting and—would you believe it?—even the teenagers with more than a year's abstinence said the same thing! New recovery's too vulnerable; emotional highs and lows are dangerous territory. (Under every skirt there's a slip!).

I didn't like to hear it, but I guess I'd better listen. I can afford to wait until my Program's more solid.

The 74th DAY

    I'd been thinking it was time to slow down on meetings, call my sponsor a little less often, put aside Program literature for awhile – just give myself a chance to relax.

    Then I heard someone say we must be *willing to go to any lengths* for our recovery. *It doesn't just happen. We <u>make</u> it happen.*

IT'S A PROGRAM OF ACTION!

The 75th DAY

I've noticed there are meetings just for women, or men, or the dually-addicted, for gays or young people or professionals. If I have a particular issue to deal with, one of these meetings would be good for me, my sponsor says.

But my home group should be just an ordinary meeting, so I don't begin to think of myself as "special." I'm learning that's a character defect for a lot of addicts.

I'M NOT UNIQUE!

The 76th DAY

I don't know everyone that I see at meetings. I never see them *except* at meetings. They're not personal friends, but I have a special feeling about them. When we're all in the same room for the same reason, something happens. Is it because I trust them to be honest? I know I draw strength from them, even if they remain strangers. I know I need the Fellowship.

My sponsor says,

**TALK TO SOMEONE
I DON'T KNOW
AT EVERY MEETING.**

The 77th DAY

I've been hearing that I damaged my brain just a little, every time I used and abused something. My sponsor says not to worry; it's what I do with what's left that counts.

**ACCENTUATE the POSITIVE
with an ATTITUDE
of GRATITUDE!**

The 78th DAY

I have a lot more free time than I used to have when I was drugging—and I need to fill that time with healthy things.

My sponsor suggests that I

READ SOME PROGRAM LITERATURE EVERY DAY.

But I'm not to over-do it. A chapter of the Big Book, a daily meditation and perhaps a pamphlet are plenty for right now. I still have such a short attention span!

The 79th DAY

I think I have plenty of good ideas about the Program, and good advice for other newcomers, too. My sponsor tells me I need to do more listening. Old-timers have a tough way of reminding me that I still don't know a thing about recovery:

TAKE THE COTTON OUT OF YOUR EARS AND PUT IT IN YOUR MOUTH!

The 80th DAY

The Steps and the meetings and sponsorship aren't just therapy; they're a *way of life*. I'm trying to soak up as much knowledge as fast as I can by hanging around Program people. In fact, some of the best times are after meetings, when several of us go out together for something to eat. We joke that

WE NEED A LITTLE "DINER THERAPY."

The 81st DAY

The best therapy in the world, my sponsor says, is *daily interaction with my fellow human beings*. And that doesn't mean just meetings.

When the Program was new, (before inflation!) a sponsor might give a newcomer a meeting list with a dime taped to it, remarking:

DON'T FORGET THE IMPORTANCE OF "DIME THERAPY."

Somehow it doesn't sound right to say "quarter therapy," does it? But the message is still the same: *Use the phone; it's part of recovery.*

The 82nd DAY

It's amazing how much you can learn from Program people, just by asking one simple question!

Mostly they share their own experience, and they usually make suggestions rather than giving advice. As they say in meetings,

TAKE WHAT YOU WANT AND LEAVE THE REST.

But my sponsor likes to add that the part I most want to leave is the part I most need to take!

The 83rd DAY

IT'S THE FIRST DRINK THAT GETS YOU DRUNK!

I thought that was absurd when I first heard it, because my tolerance for alcohol and drugs was so high that it took several of *anything* before I felt it.

I guess I'm what they call a slow learner, but I finally understood when they asked me to imagine getting drunk or high *WITHOUT taking the first one!*

The 84th DAY

I think I've hit my "bottom." My sponsor says that a *bottom* isn't a place or a situation, like going to jail or losing a family; it's a *decision* to go to any lengths to turn my life all the way around and get clean and sober.

All I know is that

I'M SICK AND TIRED OF BEING SICK AND TIRED.

The 85th DAY

Whenever I begin to feel down or discouraged, I make a mental list of all the things I'm grateful for.

My sponsor suggested I write it down and call it My Gratitude List. It's impossible to feel depressed and grateful at the same time!

These days, more and more, I'm maintaining

AN ATTITUDE OF GRATITUDE.

(Can't repeat this too often!)

The 86ᵗʰ DAY

The Second Step tells me that

A POWER GREATER THAN MYSELF CAN RESTORE ME TO SANITY.

I knew that I was a bit off-balance, but "insanity" is a pretty tough word!

Then my sponsor pointed out that we all did crazy things over and over again, always *expecting a different result*. Yes, that IS insane!

The 87th DAY

My sponsor suggests that I ask my family to attend a Twelve Step group like Al-Anon for families and friends, because

THE FAMILY IS SICK TOO.

Of course I don't have to say it quite like that, but the truth is they've become sick trying for so long to adjust to my unacceptable behavior – to "fix the unfixable."

Right now they don't want much to do with me, and I can't blame them!

My sponsor says to keep working on *me*, and things are bound to change.

The 88th DAY

I'm still clean, sober and abstinent after all these days. It's hard to believe I've come such a long way, and I'm beginning to understand I have a long, long way to go.

My sponsor gets this big grin, gives me a hug and tells me to

EXPECT MIRACLES!

The 89th DAY

Tomorrow will be my ninetieth day sober, clean and serene.

My sponsor says it's important for me to celebrate with my group. I used to think celebrating was kind of silly, like a kid's birthday party. Now I know I'm a brand new kid celebrating a brand new life!

It's not just for me, but for the newcomers too, so they'll know that the Program works.

Someone is celebrating two years tomorrow, and someone else as fourteen. That hardly seems possible to me, but it's living proof that

WE CAN DO TOGETHER WHAT WE CAN'T DO ALONE!

The 90th DAY

THE PROMISES*

If we are painstaking about this phase of our development, we will be amazed before we are halfway through. We will be amazed before we are halfway through. We are going to know a new freedom and a new happiness. We will not regret the past nor wish to shut the door on it. We will comprehend the word serenity and we will know peace. No matter how far down the scale we have gone, we will see how our experience will benefit others. That feeling of uselessness and self-pity will disappear. We will lose interest in selfish things and gain interest in our fellows. Self-seeking will slip away. Our whole attitude and outlook upon life will change. Fear of people and of economic insecurity will leave us. We will intuitively know how to handle situations which used to baffle us. We will suddenly realize that God is doing for us what we could not do for ourselves.

Are these extravagant promises?

We think not.

They are being fulfilled among us—sometimes quickly, sometimes slowly. They will always materialize if we work for them.*

*Pages 83-84; *Alcoholics Anonymous*.
  Reprinted with permission

The AUTHOR

is a recovering alcoholic who found Alcoholics Anonymous in New Jersey in 1970. She moved to Maine in 1996, and has maintained long-term sobriety within the Program with the help of several close long-term sober friends, some astonishing "pigeons," (old-timer name for Sponsee) and a "Sobriety Plan" as recommended years ago by the people in the Program who favored writing things down because our brains were too mocus to remember.

JK'S SOBRIETY PLAN

1.
Don't Drink or drug and go to meetings.

2.
2 meetings <u>minimum</u>/week,
One a Step meeting.

3.
<u>Ride</u> with someone if possible.

4.
Stick with the winners.

5.
At each meeting, speak to
someone I don't usually talk to.

6.
Avoid sugar, OTC and Rx meds.
(Rx emergency only!)

7.
Greet HP with thanks in AM.

8.
Do inventory and thank HP PM.

9.
Communicate with an AA daily.

10.
Pray and meditate daily.

11.
Say "thank you" often.
Read the Promises (page 83-84)

12.
Live the Steps
Special attention to Steps 10, 11, 12

▲

*Doing less than 5 regularly?
Danger!!!*

Thoughts from my Sponsor

Len K. explained that alcoholism is a *thinking* problem. When he was drunk, the logic of his active disease was impeccable:

> ***"Aristotle is a man;***
> ***All men are mortal.***
> ***Therefore it's okay***
> ***to drink <u>now</u>!"***

Early on, he also asked me,

"What is a sponsor's primary responsibility?"

(next page)

BE SOBER!

Made in the USA
Middletown, DE
29 May 2016